MW01132935

to my sister,

By Eden Willow

to my sister, Copyright © 2024 By Eden Willow.
All rights reserved.
No part of this publication may be reproduced, distributed, or transmitted in any
form or by any means, including photocopying, recording, or other electronic or
mechanical methods, without the prior written permission of the publisher, except in
the case of brief quotations embodied in critical reviews and certain other non-
commercial uses permitted by copyright law.

introduction

to my dearest sister,

in these pages lies more than just words; it's a heartfelt tribute to you, my sister – my confidante, my ally, my irreplaceable sibling.

you are the keeper of our shared memories, the co-author of our childhood stories, and the unwavering supporter in the journey of life that lies ahead.

this book is a daily reminder of my profound affection for you.

over the next 100 days, may each page greet you with warmth and joy each morning.

contained within are words of love, beams of hope, and reflections of the remarkable person you are.

consider this a daily embrace, a token of my admiration, and a reminder of your remarkable resilience and grace.

you are a beacon of light in my world, a truly exceptional soul, and i want these pages to echo the love and pride i feel for you every day.

forever in my heart,

to my sister

DAY #1

you have a way of making everything brighter, of turning ordinary moments into memories.

i cherish every second spent with you.

your spirit is a gift to those lucky enough to know you.

to my sister

DAY #2

seeing you face life's hurdles with such empathy and
understanding for others, even when you are going through
your own storms, is truly inspiring.

it reminds me of the incredible person you are.

to my sister

DAY #3

in the garden of life, you're the most radiant flower.

your love and warmth nurture my soul.

to my sister

DAY #4

remember, i am your anchor in any storm and your cheerleader in every victory.

we're in this together, always.

to my sister

DAY #5

in you, i find a confidante, a partner in crime, a soul so kind, in a world so unkind.

our shared memories, a tapestry of love and laughter, binding us closer, in this chapter and ever after.

to my sister

DAY #6

in every step you take, i'll be right beside you, cheering you on.

remember, my support for you is as endless as the sky.

to my sister

DAY #7

your strength is a beacon that lights up even my darkest days.

seeing you conquer every challenge with grace and determination is a constant reminder of the incredible person you are.

to my sister

DAY #8

i still remember your comforting embrace during my hardest times, your laughter in my happiest moments.

you've been my rock, my joy, and my greatest support.

our bond is a beautiful dance of love and friendship.

to my sister

DAY #*9*

life gave me a sister, but in you, i found a hero.

your courage, your wisdom, and your kindness shape my world in ways you can't imagine.

i am forever grateful for you.

to my sister

DAY #*10*

you are not alone in this vast world.

i am with you, in every step, every struggle, your silent guardian and greatest supporter.

to my sister

DAY #11

you are never alone in your journey.

i am here, a constant presence, ready to offer a shoulder, an ear,
or a helping hand.

to my sister

DAY *#12*

your resilience astounds me, facing life with grace and poise.

in every challenge, you find a voice.

a voice that comforts, that fights, that loves, a sister like you is a blessing from above.

to my sister

DAY #*13*

your laughter is a reminder that happiness is a choice.

may you always find reasons to smile and paths that lead to your dreams.

to my sister

DAY #14

from stealing cookies from the kitchen to conquering the biggest challenges in life, we've done it all together.

you've been my partner in every mischief and my support in every sorrow.

our bond is unbreakable and it only grows stronger with each passing day.

to my sister

DAY #*15*

your journey may be tough, but it's also beautiful, just like you.

keep moving forward, i am right beside you every step of the way.

to my sister

DAY #*16*

in every laughter, every tear, and every triumph, you've been there, shining brightly.

you're not only strong and compassionate, but you also have the rare gift of making everyone around you feel special.

to my sister

DAY #*17*

in the toughest of times, remember our shared laughter and joy.

those memories are a testament to your wonderful spirit, a spirit that can overcome anything.

to my sister

DAY #*18*

it's not just about the heights you've reached, but the depths
you've explored within yourself.

your journey of self-discovery and growth has been nothing
short of inspiring.

to my sister

DAY #*19*

from childhood giggles to adult dreams, we've woven a tapestry
of shared memories.

your support, a constant in my ever-changing world, your love,
a treasure, more precious than pearls.

to my sister

DAY *#20*

in your smile, i find peace, in your embrace, a home.

with you, i've never felt alone.

your presence is a gift, a light in my life, in moments of joy and strife.

DAY #*21*

your presence in my life is like a gentle, steady flame that lights up the darkest of days.

you have a heart of gold, and your love and care have been my sanctuary.

DAY *#22*

even when we're miles apart, i feel your presence with me,
guiding and supporting me like you always have.

our bond transcends distance and time, a testament to the
incredible sisterhood we share.

to my sister

DAY #23

every time i think about you, i am reminded of the light you
bring into my life.

your laughter, your kindness, and your unwavering support.

you're not just my sister; you're my guiding star.

to my sister

DAY *#24*

in every challenge you face, remember you have the strength to overcome it.

your resilience shines brighter than you realise, and i am here, always cheering you on.

to my sister

DAY #25

you've always had this amazing ability to rise from challenges, stronger and wiser.

watching your journey, your growth, has been a lesson in resilience and grace.

to my sister

DAY #26

in the quiet moments, i reflect on our bond, a connection so profound.

your laughter, a balm to my soul, your wisdom, making me whole.

to my sister

DAY #27

for every tear you've wiped, every laugh we've shared, and every moment you've been there, thank you.

you're not just a sister, but a true friend and an irreplaceable part of my life.

to my sister

DAY *#28*

life's journey is tough, but so are you.

you've faced every storm with courage and grace.

never forget how incredible that makes you.

to my sister

DAY #29

i admire your ability to see beauty in everything and everyone.

your optimistic spirit is contagious, and it's one of the many reasons why i feel so blessed to call you my sister.

to my sister

DAY #*30*

the empathy you show to others, even when you're facing your
own battles, is a testament to your beautiful heart.

remember, i'm here to offer that same empathy and
understanding to you, whenever you need it.

to my sister

DAY #*31*

your journey hasn't been easy, yet you've faced it all with a
smile and a heart full of hope.

your unwavering spirit and positive outlook are things i admire
the most about you.

you are the epitome of strength and grace.

to my sister

DAY *#32*

your journey of personal growth has been like watching a
flower bloom in slow motion – beautiful, gradual, and awe-
inspiring.

every stage more magnificent than the last.

DAY #*33*

life's journey is tough, but having you by my side makes every step worth it.

your strength is my strength, your happiness, my happiness.

to my sister

DAY #34

when you feel like giving up, remember why you started.

you have a world of potential inside you, and i can't wait to see
all that you accomplish.

to my sister

DAY *#35*

remember how we used to dream about the future?

now, as i look back, i realise our greatest adventures weren't those grand plans, but the everyday moments we shared.

those are the true treasures of our life together.

to my sister

DAY #*36*

remember, the stars can't shine without darkness.

you've shown me that resilience and grace can turn struggles
into stars.

DAY #37

i still laugh thinking about our childhood antics, the pranks we played, and the countless hours of fun we had.

those memories are my treasure, a reminder of the pure joy and love we share.

thank you for filling my life with laughter and warmth.

to my sister

DAY *#38*

your kindness is a ripple that touches so many lives, including mine.

you don't just make a difference, you are the difference.

to my sister

DAY #*39*

like a phoenix, you rise from the ashes, stronger and more beautiful.

your resilience is a beacon of hope that lights my way.

to my sister

DAY *#40*

we've shared memories, secrets, and dreams.

my commitment to supporting you is as deep as the bond we share.

to my sister

DAY #41

life is a beautiful journey, and i'm grateful to walk it with you.

i'm excited to see all the amazing places you'll go and the incredible things you'll do.

to my sister

DAY #42

our shared secrets, whispered in the dark, our adventures, wild
and stark.

you, my sister, my heart's counterpart, together, we've crafted a
work of art.

to my sister

DAY *#43*

in this vast tapestry of life, your thread is the most vibrant.

your courage, your laughter, they weave joy into my days.

to my sister

DAY *#44*

you've always been the one to light up a room and inspire
others to follow their hearts.

keep being that beacon of hope and joy, it's your greatest gift.

to my sister

DAY #45

in your eyes, i see a spark that lights up the darkest rooms.

keep shining, keep dreaming, and know that i'll always be here cheering you on.

to my sister

DAY #46

your light shines so brightly, it guides me through my darkest days.

you're not just my sister, you're my lighthouse in the storm.

to my sister

DAY #47

your resilience in the face of adversity is nothing short of remarkable.

it's not just about what you've achieved, but how you've uplifted others along the way.

you are truly an extraordinary soul.

to my sister

DAY #48

your dreams are not out of reach; they are just waiting for you to catch up.

keep pushing, keep striving, because i know you can achieve anything.

to my sister

DAY #49

the grace with which you handle every situation, turning
challenges into opportunities for growth, is truly inspiring.

you are not only a wonderful sister but a remarkable human
being.

to my sister

DAY #50

no matter the distance, time zone, or circumstance, my help
and heart are always just a phone call away.

you never have to face anything alone.

to my sister

DAY #*51*

i've watched you grow, overcome, and thrive.

know this - i am here, always ready to listen, laugh, and lend a hand.

to my sister

DAY #52

remember the strength that lies within you.

it's a force that can move mountains and break barriers.

you've got this, and i've got you.

to my sister

DAY #53

as we walked life's winding roads, you were always there, a beacon of strength and love.

your wisdom, kindness, and unwavering support have shaped me in ways i can't express.

i am eternally grateful for the gift of you in my life.

to my sister

DAY #54

through every challenge, remember my unwavering faith in you.

i see your strength, even on days when you don't.

to my sister

DAY #55

every step of your journey has added to the beautiful tapestry of who you are.

from every fall, you've risen; from every setback, you've learned.

your growth is a story of triumph and tenacity.

to my sister

DAY *#56*

through thick and thin, we've journeyed together, an
unbreakable bond that time nor distance can sever.

your laughter, a melody that brightens my darkest days, your
strength, an anchor in life's unpredictable waves.

to my sister

DAY #57

every step you take towards your dreams fills me with such
pride.

remember, the sky's not the limit, it's just the view.

keep reaching for those stars.

to my sister

DAY #58

with you, i've shared my deepest secrets and my highest highs.

you've been my confidant, my partner in crime, and my pillar of strength.

thank you for being my everything.

to my sister

DAY *#59*

in every challenge you face, i see the strength and courage that defines you.

even when the path gets tough, remember, i am always here, walking beside you, ready to listen, support, and share your journey, no matter where it takes us.

to my sister

DAY #60

remember when we were kids and you had those big dreams?

seeing you chase them, adapt, and grow into the person you are today fills me with immense pride.

your journey is a testament to your courage and determination.

to my sister

DAY #61

you've turned every obstacle into a stepping stone towards your growth.

it's incredible to see how far you've come, evolving into the amazing person you are today.

to my sister

DAY *#62*

the way we could communicate with just a look, our inside jokes, the way you always knew what i needed to hear.

these are the threads that weave the tapestry of our unique bond.

i'm grateful for every little thing that makes us, us.

to my sister

DAY *#63*

life's twists and turns can't break us.

i'm here, through thick and thin, always ready to support you
with all my heart.

to my sister

DAY #64

your kindness is a rare gem in this world.

the way you care, the way you love, and the way you give - it all
makes you not just my sister, but a guiding light in my life.

DAY #65

there is no obstacle too big for you to conquer.

i've seen you triumph over challenges before, and i have no doubt you'll do it again.

to my sister

DAY #66

your courage inspires me.

no matter what comes your way, i'll be standing with you, every step of the way.

to my sister

DAY #67

remember, after every storm comes a rainbow.

no matter what life throws your way, you've got the grit and grace to turn challenges into triumphs.

to my sister

DAY #68

life hasn't always been easy, but watching you navigate your struggles with such dignity has taught me so much.

you've shown me the true meaning of bravery and compassion.

to my sister

DAY #69

your struggles have not gone unnoticed.

i see your resilience, your grace under pressure, and your unyielding strength.

know that in your moments of doubt, you have my unwavering support and love.

to my sister

DAY #70

remember those late night talks we used to have, the ones
where we'd plan our future and share our deepest secrets?

those moments are etched in my heart forever.

you've always been more than a sister to me, you're my
confidante, my partner in crime, my best friend.

to my sister

DAY #71

i've seen you grow, fall, rise, and conquer.

your journey is a testament to the power of optimism.

keep that spirit alive, it's contagious.

to my sister

DAY #72

you have this incredible ability to turn challenges into
opportunities.

your resilience and optimism have taught me so much.

you are not just my sister but my role model.

to my sister

DAY #73

in the tapestry of life, you're the brightest thread, weaving joy
and hope into our family fabric.

keep colouring our world with your vibrant dreams.

to my sister

DAY #74

in every phase of your life, you've grown in ways that amaze
me.

your strength, your wisdom, your kindness – they all shine
brighter with each passing year.

to my sister

DAY #75

watching you grow has been one of the greatest joys of my life.

every challenge you've faced, you've overcome with grace and strength.

your resilience inspires me every day.

to my sister

DAY #76

the way you chase your dreams with fierce determination and
unwavering passion is a sight to behold.

you've turned the impossible into possible, and that's
something that fills my heart with immense pride.

to my sister

DAY #77

in the tapestry of my life, your colors are the most vibrant.

you add love, joy, and so much laughter.

thank you for being the best part of my every day.

to my sister

DAY #78

the way you embrace life's ups and downs teaches me to find
beauty in every moment.

you turn life's simple pleasures into cherished memories.

DAY #*79*

you've blossomed in ways i never imagined possible.

from the little sister who followed me around to the incredible woman you are today, your growth has been a beautiful journey to witness.

to my sister

DAY *#80*

your courage inspires me, a beacon of hope in stormy seas.

in your eyes, i see the reflection of the best in me.

together, we are invincible, an unyielding team, you and me.

to my sister

DAY #*81*

from the way you turn obstacles into stepping stones to how
you spread kindness wherever you go, you're not just my sister,
you're my hero.

witnessing your journey and growth fills me with awe.

to my sister

DAY *#82*

there's a comfort in knowing that you've been with me through every phase of life.

from those awkward teenage years to the challenges of adulthood, you've been my constant.

i am who i am because of your love and guidance.

to my sister

DAY #83

life can be a rollercoaster, but i promise to ride every high and low with you.

you've got a permanent partner in me.

to my sister

DAY *#84*

you're the melody in life's symphony, adding rhythm and
harmony to my world.

your presence is a song that uplifts my spirit.

to my sister

DAY #85

remember, the stars can't shine without darkness.

in your moments of doubt, know that you are capable of
creating your own light.

i believe in you, endlessly.

to my sister

DAY #86

watching you grow and evolve into the person you are today
has been one of the greatest joys of my life.

your journey is a testament to your strength, and i admire you
more than words can express.

to my sister

DAY #87

i marvel at your ability to face life's storms with such courage and poise.

you're not just surviving; you're thriving, and in doing so, you inspire me every single day.

90

to my sister

DAY *#88*

it's not just the happy days that have strengthened our bond,
but the days when you've struggled and i've been there to hold
your hand.

your vulnerability is not a weakness; it's a gift that brings us
closer.

to my sister

DAY *#89*

your resilience astounds me.

the way you handle life's ups and downs with such grace and
determination is something i admire deeply.

you're not just my sister; you're a beacon of hope and a
reminder that we can get through anything together.

to my sister

DAY #*90*

life has thrown its challenges, but you've faced them with a
courage that's awe-inspiring.

your growth, through all these experiences, has been a joy to
witness.

to my sister

DAY *#91*

your strength is awe-inspiring.

the way you handle life's ups and downs with such grace,
always with a smile.

you are the embodiment of resilience and love, and i admire
you more than words can say.

to my sister

DAY *#92*

life has its ups and downs, but one thing remains true.

having you as my sister, is the best, through and through.

in every smile, every tear, our bond is a treasure, so incredibly dear.

to my sister

DAY #*93*

your journey hasn't been an easy one, yet you face each day with such positivity and grace.

know that i am always here, cheering you on and ready to support you in any way i can.

to my sister

DAY #94

you've faced so many challenges, yet you never let them dim your spirit.

your courage in the face of adversity is a constant source of inspiration to me.

remember, in your moments of struggle, my admiration and support for you only grow stronger.

to my sister

DAY *#95*

your strength is an unspoken promise of hope to everyone around you.

never doubt the power of your own resilience.

i believe in you, today and always.

to my sister

DAY #*96*

your ability to rise every time you fall is something i not only admire but strive to emulate.

in your moments of doubt, remember, i am always here, proud to call you my sister and ready to offer a shoulder or an ear, whichever you need more.

to my sister

DAY #97

you are my compass, always guiding me back to what matters
most.

your wisdom is a treasure, a gift that enriches my life.

to my sister

DAY *#98*

with every challenge you face, you emerge stronger and wiser.

your journey is a beacon of hope, reminding us all that the best is yet to come.

to my sister

DAY #99

do you remember the time we got lost on our way home and ended up having the adventure of a lifetime?

that day taught me that with you by my side, even the most uncertain paths can lead to beautiful destinations.

i cherish every second of our shared journeys.

to my sister

DAY #*100*

as we've grown, our paths may diverge, but our bond remains a constant urge.

in you, i see a reflection of myself, a bond deeper than anything else.

Made in the USA
Coppell, TX
29 April 2024

31815065R00059